Twist and Shout!

Copyright © 2017 Brett Fleishman. All rights reserved.

This is a work of fiction. Names, characters, places and incidents are products of the author's imagination or are used fictitiously and should not be construed as real. Any resemblance to actual events, locales, organizations or persons, living or dead, is entirely coincidental.

No part of this book may be used or reproduced in any manner whatsoever without written permission, except in the case of brief quotations embodied in critical articles and reviews. For more information, e-mail all inquiries to info@mindstirmedia.com.

Published by Mindstir Media LLC

45 Lafayette Rd. Suite 181 | North Hampton, NH 03862 | USA

1.800.767.0531 | www.mindstirmedia.com

ISBN-13: 978-0-9993872-0-7

Library of Congress Control Number: 2017913714

This book is dedicated to Dylan...
Nobody makes me laugh more than you do

Jordan,

"Always dream big.
It's OK if you do.
If you don't there's no way
That your dream will come true."

Brett Fleishman

Wordplays

I love using wordplays in my poems. My favorite wordplays are puns and idioms. If you don't know what puns and idioms are, that's OK. I define them in the appendix of this book. I also explain, poem by poem, what makes these puns and idioms funny (well, funny to me, that is).

How will you know whether the poem has a pun or an idiom in it? Great question!

If you see (P) at the end of the poem, it means there is a pun at the end of the poem. If you see (I) at the end of the poem, it means there is an idiom at the end of the poem. If you don't see either, it means the poem doesn't have a pun or an idiom in it.

Got it? Good! Come on in...

Table of Contents

1. POEM 1
2. FIDGETY LANCE
3. 20 BUCKS
4. BOY NICKNAMES
5. TWO-LETTER SOUP?
6. KEVIN THE INHALER
7. DOVE LOVE
8. ZANY WORD BLENDER #1
9. EVERYDAY FEELINGS
10. MY REPORT CARD
11. FAIRLY UNFAIR FAIR
12. SAME NAME
13. IT'S ONLY MILK
14. IF THE SHOE DOESN'T FIT…
15. LEFT FIELDER JALEN
16. OBSTACLES
17. ROVER'S BACKYARD

SECRET POEM - I'm a secret poem. You were NOT supposed to

18. ZANY WORD BLENDER #2
19. NAP TIME
20. GAME OF CARDS
21. PRETZEL MAN
22. SECOND-HAND BIKE
23. SIMPLE MATH RIDDLE?
24. CAVEMAN'S CONQUEST
25. ZANY WORD BLENDER #3
26. STEAK-ING HER CLAIM
27. TAYLOR
28. TWIST AND SHOUT!
29. CIRCUS SHMIRCUS
30. WINDOW SHOPPING
31. WORKING THE BOWLADROME
32. MONEY-MAKING $CHEME
33. ALPHABET CATCHER

find me! Please do not tell anyone. For that, I thank you kindly.

POEM 1

Poem 1 must be the best
Since it's the first you'll read
It should rhyme and make you laugh
I'm sure those things you need
If you think this poem's lame
Don't give it one more look
Mom has tons of chores for you...
Oh, **now** you'll read this book?!

FIDGETY LANCE

Outside, in this garden, lives fidgety Lance
Who, for more than a week, has been sleeping on plants
For the first seven days, he seemed dazed, in a trance
He was clueless that week and did not see the ants
Then, on Day Number 8, the boy took a quick glance
At his legs and his arms, where those ants did advance
Lance jumped up, right away, in a very firm stance
There he waved his arms wildly. What a strange dance!
But the ants didn't leave, and it wasn't by chance
Poor Lance couldn't stay calm with those ants in his pants [1]

20 BUCKS

Ethan offered 20 bucks
To any friend who knew
Answers to four questions
He did not give them a clue

'What's a state that starts with K?
Who knows what's 10 times three?
What's another word for fast?
Can anyone spell spree?'

Sammy gave the first response
She blurted instantly:
'Kansas, 40, blistering
And s-p-r-e-e'

Next to go was Anderson
He answered right away:
'Kansas, 30, blistering
And s-p-r-e-a'

At the end went Isabelle
She whispered timidly:
'Kansas, 30, blistering
And s-p-r-e-e'

Once all three friends answered
Ethan told them one was right
'Isabelle's our champion!'
She jumped up with delight

Isabelle could not believe
She'd just won 20 bucks
In the distance, then she saw
A bunch of giant trucks

They stopped next to Isabelle
The doors rose from the rear
Ethan kept his promise
Soon came out the 20 deer [P]

BOY NICKNAMES

Many boys like nicknames
They think names sound better short
This is true for Mortimer
His close friends call him Mort

Daniel hasn't used his name in years
He goes by Dan
Stanley won't respond
Unless a person calls him Stan

Frederick's fine with Freddy
He is also fine with Fred
Theodore does not reply
To anything but Ted

Only one boy doesn't like his nickname
This is true
It makes Stewart anxious
Yes, his nickname makes him Stew [P]

TWO-LETTER SOUP?

They make alphabet soup
Every day at this store
From 11:15
Until 6:34

And what makes this store great
And extremely unique
Are the letters they put
In their soup every week

They don't use all the letters
They only use two
And since each week they switch
They're exciting and new

Yet despite all this fun
Sales have slowed recently
It began weeks ago
With the soup *F&T*

And last week wasn't great
Soup sales didn't do well
Grumpy customers didn't
Like soup *G&L*

With soup sales in a funk
The store owners approve
An idea they believe
Will help sales to improve

They will add a third letter
'Two isn't enough!'
But which letters?
They know this decision is tough

They agree on the O
They decide on the A
They debate a few letters
But then choose the K

Word spreads quickly through town
Of this three-letter soup
Lots of people line up
It's a very large group

Yes, their new idea works
Sales are way up today
Life is better again
Things are now A-OK [1]

KEVIN THE INHALER

When he was a little boy
Poor Kevin couldn't breathe
Not as well as other kids
That's what he did believe

When he lay in bed to sleep
He'd sometimes gasp and cough
Medicines did not work well
They quickly did wear off

Kevin met a doctor
Who had seen this all before
'Try this new inhaler
Twice a day but never more'

Kevin used it twice a day
His symptoms did improve
Next, he tried three times a day
This was a foolish move

It turns out three times a day
Was simply too demanding
Kevin's belt felt very small
His body was expanding

Kevin's swollen ankles
Couldn't fit inside his boots
Kevin's bloated shoulders
Ripped the seams off Kevin's suits

Once he realized his mistake
The medicines he stopped
But it was too late
Yes, on that day, poor Kevin popped

DOVE LOVE

When the world's shyest goose
Sees the world's cutest dove
Right away, from afar
It falls madly in love

The goose wants to approach
But knows not what to say
So it stays in the distance
And watches each day

Then one day not long after
The goose falls asleep
The dove sits by the goose
But does not say a peep

When the goose sees the dove
Very startled it jumps
It's completely embarrassed
And full of goose bumps [1]

ZANY WORD BLENDER #1
(things you wear)

Gabby loves turkey and ham   _____

Thomas and Alex eat jam   _____

Annabel tries the fish   _____

Which, at times, tastes delish _____

Aaron eats classic oatmeal with lamb _____

*Inside each line, I hi**d one** word*

*Combi**ne t**hem since, right now, they're blurred*

EVERYDAY FEELINGS

Mondays make Manny feel mostly mysterious
Tuesdays make Tina feel totally tedious

Wednesdays make Wendy feel wishful and willing
Thursdays make Theo feel thoughtful and thrilling

Fridays make Freddy feel fiendishly freaky
Saturdays make Sarah feel super sneaky

Which of these days makes you feel most complete?
I prefer Sundaes. They make me feel sweet. [P]

MY REPORT CARD

Dad opened my report card
After work the other day
He saw three *F's* and then three *D's*
But not one *B* or *A*

Dad rubbed his fingers on his head
As if he were in pain
He said, 'These grades are terrible.
I need you to explain'

So I explained to dear old Dad
'An *A* means *Awful Work*.
Of course, I didn't get an A'
(I tried hard not to smirk)

Dad looked confused as I went on
'A *B* means *Badly Done*.
There's no way I would get a *B*
Because I worked a ton'

I focused on my top three grades
'A *D* means *Dynamite*.
It's no surprise I did so well
I studied every night'

And then I let my father know
'An *F* stands for *First-Rate*.
I knew I'd get a lot of *F's*
My teachers say I'm great'

Dad calmly turned to me and said
'Nice effort, son, well played.
Make sure you work as hard next year
When you repeat third grade'

Fairly Unfair Fair

Paula the Pickle and Peter the Pear
Meet Tom the Tomato today at the fair

Peter wolfs down three large scoops of ice cream
Paula has none so, upset, she does steam

Paula plays games. She wins prize after prize.
Peter, who's losing, gives her evil eyes

Watching while Peter and Paula are jealous
Tom remains calm. He does not appear zealous.

Tom the Tomato shows them both respect
He is *not* green with envy as you might expect [1]

SAME NAME

Ella finished boarding school
Then met her one true love
Matthew Vader was his name
He fit her like a glove

Matthew was the sweetest guy
He took great care of Ella
When it rained he'd flip his coat
To make her an umbrella

Proud to be her guy
Excited, Matthew soon proposed
Ella shouted, 'Yes!'
The girl could hardly stay composed

Just before their wedding
Ella said something in shame
She told Matthew
'I would really like to keep my name'

Seeing Matthew frown
The girl felt like a giant traitor
But she had no choice
She couldn't end up Ella Vader

Matthew later understood
Her name looked strange in print
He told Ella, 'Keep your name'
So she stayed Ella Fint

IT'S ONLY MILK

Morgan loves her milk
But only drinks milk when it's chilled
Soon her cup falls down
Before it was completely filled
Mom tells Morgan, 'Clean your mess!'
Her Mom does not look thrilled
Morgan's not upset
And won't cry over milk that spilled [1]

IF THE SHOE DOESN'T FIT...

Dawn is not an early riser
Rich is such a stingy miser

Ernest? He is insincere.
Sandy hates the beach I hear

Valentine says she won't date
Victor loses 15 straight

August smiles when it's cold
Walker always sits I'm told

Tiger is extremely weak
Hope? She knows her outlook's bleak.

Mason doesn't like to build
Faith has never felt fulfilled

Frank deceives. He's full of lies.
Angel flashes evil eyes

Still, Moms love them just the same
No big deal, what's in a name? (P)

LEFT FIELDER JALEN

The game starts off normally at the beginning
Then something strange happens in the third inning

Once the umpire shouts out, 'Let's play ball!'
The first batter, confused, finds no home plate at all

Right in front of the catcher, not far from his face
Sits a large clump of dirt where there once was a base

Someone's taken home plate! It's clear this base was stolen!
Who stole the plate? Brady, Jalen or Nolan?

Turns out that Jalen's not manning left field
He is off to the side, near the stands, well-concealed

Yes, he's sitting alone off in foul territory
(Why is this Jalen a part of this story?)

Underneath Jalen, of course, is home plate
Yes, he *did* steal the base. That's not up for debate.

Once the ballgame resumes, after this brief delay
Jalen's stuck on the bench, punished for his foul play [1]

Obstacles

Pretend you couldn't walk at all
Or even drive a car
Could you still be President?
Of course, like FDR!

Pretend you couldn't see one bit
The moment you were born
Could you be a swimming star?
Of course, like Trischa Zorn!

Pretend you couldn't see or hear
A fate that isn't stellar
Could you publish books?
Of course you could, like Hellen Keller!

Obstacles are part of life
You'll surely face some too
Doesn't matter what they are
Don't let them conquer you

ROVER'S BACKYARD

Rover likes to roam outside
He has a big backyard
He can't see above the picket fences
That's too hard

Nobody will mow his lawn
Or fertilize the soil
Weeds are sprouting everywhere
This makes the dog's blood boil

Making matters worse
The neighbor's dogs play every day
Rover's sure their lawn's well-groomed
A perfect place to play

One day Rover's moping
As a storm forms all around
Soon the winds destroy his fence
It crumbles to the ground

Rover sees his neighbor's grass
But he is unimpressed
There are brown spots everywhere
This Rover hadn't guessed

Rover is surprised to learn
His backyard was much cleaner
Why was Rover jealous
Since his grass was always greener? [1]

ZANY WORD BLENDER #2
(kitchen items)

If you spot sister out late tonight _____

She may sleep late tomorrow, she might _____

She may well nap and snore _____

So appalling, for sure _____

She's not able to wake, that's not right _____

*Inside each line, I hi**d one** word*
*Combi**ne t**hem since, right now, they're blurred*

NAP TIME

Raise your hand in the air
If you think school's too long
Can't they add a quick nap?
Would that be very wrong?

I proposed this idea
Then my teacher did snap
'You're in middle school now.
You do not need to nap!'

Yes, I **do** need to nap
Afternoons I am beat
A quick snooze after recess
Would be pretty sweet

But my teacher will notice
If I close my eyes
For my plan to work out
I will need a disguise

If my eyes are still open
When I'm not awake
I can rest afternoons
When I need a short break

So I grab a few markers
(They're white, black and teal)
I draw eyes on my eyelids
They look pretty real

Not too long after recess
(10 minutes past 1)
I doze off during math class
(This class isn't fun)

When I wake from my nap
Near my head I can see
My math teacher's upset
She is staring at me

To the principal's office
I'm told I must go
But I can't figure out...
How did my teacher know?

I ask, 'How did you know
I was sleeping for sure?'
She responds, 'It was clear
When you started to snore'

GAME OF CARDS

Calvin was a gloomy boy
A pessimist for sure
He complained when things went wrong
He wasn't too mature

Sophie was a cheerful girl
Upbeat in many ways
She searched for the good in things
That's how she spent her days

These two kids lived side-by-side
They played games in their yards
One day Calvin asked his friend
To play a game of cards

Sophie said she would of course
She asked him how to play
Calvin said, 'The high score wins'
Their game was underway!

Calvin glanced down at his cards
And this is what he found:
A jack, an eight, a six, two threes
Disgusted, Calvin frowned

Sophie peeked down at her cards
They weren't quite what she'd dreamed:
A jack, an eight, a six, two threes
Despite this, Sophie beamed

Even though these kids had tied
So differently they felt
One upset and one content
With cards that they were dealt [1]

PRETZEL MAN

Though it took several long years, he persisted
This man, so strange, did his work unassisted
'I'll build the best pretzel yet,' he insisted
Quite an idea, though perhaps a bit twisted [P]

SECOND-HAND BIKE

He constructed a bike
From aluminum cans
Out of newspaper strips
And the blades of old fans
With the iron and steel
From three used frying pans
So creative, indeed, was this Michael!

Excited, he took the bike
Out for a dash
Moments later he swerved
Then there was a loud crash
It was ruined, his bike
Which he threw in the trash
He remembered, of course, to recycle

SIMPLE MATH RIDDLE?

On the ground, young Heather looks
She's shocked by what she sees
There's a 4, a couple 1's
Two 2's and then two 3's

All told there are seven numbers
Scattered on the floor
Heather must pick up just two
These two must add to four

But there is one tiny catch
She cannot choose a 1
That would be too easy
And it wouldn't be much fun

If she picks two cards correctly
Heather gets a prize
She does not know what it is
But loves a good surprise

This game seems so easy
But for Heather it is not
She does not like math
In fact, it bothers her a lot

Since she's stumped, she will not win
This is bad news for Heather
Though she tried she never could
Put 2 and 2 together [1]

CAVEMAN'S CONQUEST

After catching a dinosaur
Winning the hunt
The young caveman returned
Then he let out a grunt

When the wife of the caveman
Saw what he did slay
She jumped up and knocked over
Her curds and her whey

'I am very impressed!
You did that on your own?'
But the caveman responded
With only a groan

The wife asked
'Was the dinosaur tough to transport?'
But the caveman said nothing
Just let out a snort

The wife asked
'Was the dinosaur feisty or meek?'
But the caveman said little
Just let out a shriek

Quite annoyed, the wife cleaned up
Her whey and her curds
It was pointless engaging
This man of few words [1]

ZANY WORD BLENDER #3
(fruits)

An antelope army all clapped _____

At the poor angelfish as it napped _____

Then a male monkey scanned _____

An old camel on land _____

Who lived next to a crab that was trapped _____

*Inside each line, I hi**d one** word*

*Combi**ne t**hem since, right now, they're blurred*

STEAK-ING HER CLAIM

When the waiter brings out
The large steak on a plate
The steak looks undercooked
Unappealing to Kate

She requests that the chef
Cook her steak a bit more
'I like medium-well
As I mentioned before!'

But the waiter refuses
To take the steak back
'Let me know if you'd like me
To get my boss Jack'

Kate insists that he does
'Yes, I'll speak to your boss!'
She says this with arms folded
Kate clearly is cross

When the boss speaks to Kate
He attempts to be nice
'We won't cook your steak more
But we'll charge you half price'

Kate's disgusted the chef
Will not warm up her meal
But, although she's displeased
Kate accepts his raw deal [1]

TAYLOR

One day I met Taylor
She was sitting by the lift
She was strumming her guitar
It's clear she had a gift
I asked her to race me down
She did though she seemed miffed
She skied slowly
Why did I think Taylor would be Swift? (P)

TWIST AND SHOUT!

On the very top deck
Of this very tall ship
Lots of children play Twister
Like Angie and Kip

They are hoping to break
The world record tonight
With 100 kids on the top deck
They just might

But to win all their hands
Must be flat on the ground
On the bright-colored circles
That lie all around

If they do this together
A record they'll set
Since 100 kids haven't done
This before yet

The kids bend and they twist
On this deck, as a group
Some lean forwards, some backwards
Some crouch and some stoop

Someone counts all their hands
All 200 are there
They have broken the record
With one hand to spare!

Now they celebrate, screaming
Why not? What the heck!
They succeeded together
With all hands on deck [1]

CIRCUS SHMIRCUS

The knife thrower's not throwing knives
She's crouching all alone
The swallower put down his swords
He just let out a groan

The tightrope walker's dizzy now
I see him sitting down
The clown's not in a laughing mood
In fact, she sports a frown

The bearded lady's face is bare
Quite recently she shaved
The fire breather will not touch
The torches he once braved

The trapeze artist will not swing
Not with her fear of heights
The snake charmer's not charming snakes
He did on other nights

I'm gonna leave this big tent now
It's time I disappear
Guess I was wrong to think
There was a three-ring circus here [1]

WINDOW SHOPPING

Mom is always window shopping
She loves to explore
But we don't need windows
We could really use a door [1]

WORKING THE BOWLADROME

Kids who once worked
In this Bowladrome quit
They did not like their jobs
Didn't like them one bit

Some would not clean the shoes
They could not stand the smell
Kids like Owen and Erin
And Aaron and Elle

Some refused to stack bowling balls
On the top rack
Kids like Gracie and Colton
And Ashlyn and Jack

One would not clean the finger holes
Inside a ball
I believe it was Bailey
It may have been Paul

Two refused to wipe mud
Off the floor near Lane 9
They were twins I believe:
Anna and Caroline

There is only one kid
Who enjoys working here
She enjoys it so much
This could be her career

Yes, this Bowladrome
Seems to be perfect for Sally
She loves her job
It is right up her alley [1]

MONEY-MAKING $CHEME

My big sister has this plan
A plan without a hitch
She does chores to earn some cash
She hopes to strike it rich

I don't think she's figured out
My plan is far more stealthy
I've cut holes in all her jeans
So I will end up wealthy

ALPHABET CATCHER

The Alphabet Catcher
Is catching with ease
She's caught M's, she's caught K's
And a couple of B's
She caught most of these letters
Up here in the trees
Where, exhausted, she rests
She's now catching some Z's [1]

Brett's Bio

Brett Fleishman grew up in the suburbs of Philadelphia. In 1995, he earned his B.A. In 2001, he earned his M.B.A. At no point did he earn a roster spot in the N.B.A. Since 2001, Brett has been living with his two sons, Jacob and Dylan, in the greater Boston area. (Please note that, while Brett and his sons enjoy living in Boston, their sports allegiances remain firmly Philadelphian.)

To learn more about Brett, please check out his bio at **www.brettfleishman.com**. You can also follow him on Facebook (Funny Bone Tickling Poetry) and on Instagram (@funnyboneticklingpoetry).

Also by Brett Fleishman

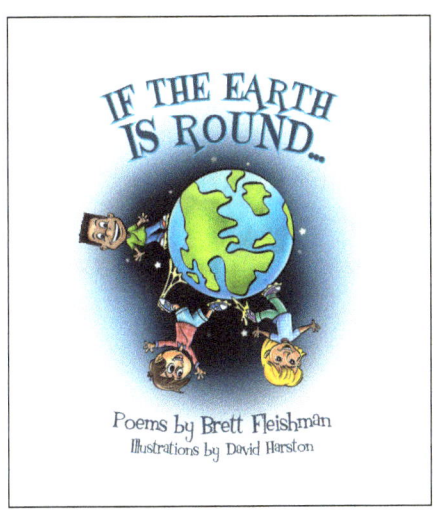

If the Earth is Round... is a compilation of 21 funny-bone-tickling poems designed for beginner readers and for adults who love reading to young children.

Empty Beaches is a compilation of 25 funny-bone-tickling poems designed for advanced readers.
Beware: this book, at times, can be extremely punny!

Appendix

Wordplays

I love to include wordplays in my poems, especially at the very end of the poems. My favorite wordplays are puns and idioms, but there are other types of wordplays, too. In case you don't know (or forget!) what puns and idioms are, here's a quick overview.

Homonyms

Wait, what? I just said we were going to review puns and idioms. Now, I'm also adding in homonyms? Not cool. I know. Not cool at all.

In order to understand what a pun is, you have to first understand what a homonym is.

A homonym is a word that is spelled one way, but has more than one meaning.

Bright is a homonym because it means either of the following:

1. Full of light
2. Intelligent

Puns

OK, so why did I make you learn about homonyms before learning about puns?

Because a pun is simply a joke that makes use of more than one meaning of a homonym.

Let's stick with the previous example. When Thomas Edison invented the light bulb, someone could have said, jokingly, 'Now, THAT was a pretty bright idea!'

Would that person have been referring to how intelligent Thomas Edison must have been to come up with a new invention? Maybe. Would that person have been referring to the brightness of the actual light bulb? Maybe. Either definition works. And that's what makes puns punny. I mean, funny.

Idioms

An idiom is a phrase that makes absolutely no sense when the words are read *literally* (exactly as described).

It's raining cats and dogs is an idiom because cats and dogs don't actually fall out of the sky when it rains. (At least not where I live, they don't!)

Yet, somehow, people realize that these nonsensical phrases have a totally different meaning. When people recognize that a nonsensical phrase has a different meaning, it means they understand the phrase *figuratively*.

Let's go back to the idiom *it's raining cats and dogs*. People recognize (somehow) that this phrase simply means, *figuratively*, that it's raining really, really hard.

I frequently include idioms at the end of my poems. What makes them funny (well, to me, at least!) is that they not only work *figuratively*, but also *literally*.

....

Is your brain hurting yet? Yeah, my brain hurts, too. Enough with the boring definitions...

What follows are explanations for all of the wordplays in this book.

POEMS WITH PUNS

20 BUCKS

Most people read the word *bucks* and think dollars. That is exactly what I wanted you to think when I wrote, at the very beginning of this poem, 'Ethan offered 20 bucks to any friend who knew...' But, the homonym *bucks* can also mean male deer. The last line of this poem reads, 'Ethan kept his promise. Soon came out the 20 deer.' Isabelle was expecting Ethan to give her a 20-dollar bill, not 20 deer. Were you also expecting a 20-dollar bill? If so, I tricked you!

BOY NICKNAMES

This is one of my favorite poems. *Stew* is not only the nickname for the full name Stewart, but *stew* also means to fret or worry about something.

EVERYDAY FEELINGS

I mentioned above that a homonym is a word that is spelled the same way, but has two different meanings. Homophones are *two words* that are spelled differently, have different meanings, but *sound* the same. This poem touches on each day of the week, one by one. However, at the end of this poem, for *Sundays*, I use the homophone *sundaes* instead.

POEMS WITH PUNS

IF THE SHOE DOESN'T FIT

This is, unquestionably, one of my punniest poems. Every kid in this poem behaves or does things in a way that is the opposite of what their name suggests. The word *earnest*, for example, means sincere (or honest). But, in this poem, the boy Ernest is *not* sincere. Tigers, of course, are very powerful animals. But, in this poem, the boy Tiger is very weak.

PRETZEL MAN

A common definition of *twisted* is when something is bent or turned out of shape. A pretzel, for example, starts off as a long, straight piece of dough before it gets twisted into a pretzel shape. Another, perhaps less common, definition of *twisted* is strange or crazy. So, in this poem, not only is the actual pretzel twisted, but the Pretzel Man's idea of making such a crazy pretzel is also a bit twisted.

TAYLOR

This poem uses a wordplay on Taylor's last name. *Swift* means able to move with great speed. In this poem, Taylor loses the race because it takes her longer to ski down the mountain. So, Taylor is NOT so *swift* after all!

POEMS WITH IDIOMS

FIDGETY LANCE

The idiom *ants in your pants* means nervous or anxious. The last line of this poem reads: 'Poor Lance couldn't stay calm with those *ants in his pants*.' This idiom works because, figuratively, Lance felt nervous about his situation. But, this phrase also works literally since Lance actually *did* have ants in his pants.

TWO-LETTER SOUP?

The idiom *A-OK* means absolutely fine. When the store owners make alphabet soup with just two letters in them, they do not sell a lot of soup. Things are not going well for them. Things are *not A-OK*. However, once the store owners add a third letter to their soup, sales increase significantly. At this point, things are going much better, so things are *A-OK*. Of course, the three letters in their soup, literally, are the letters A, O, and K.

DOVE LOVE

If you have *goose bumps*, it means you have bumps on your skin. These bumps appear when you are excited, nervous, or cold. In this poem, the goose is in love with the dove, but the goose is too shy (nervous) to approach the dove. Not surprisingly, the goose is completely startled when it awakens and sees the dove sitting nearby. This goose is embarrassed by this so, both literally and figuratively, the goose ends up with goose bumps.

POEMS WITH IDIOMS

FAIRLY UNFAIR FAIR

If you are *green with envy*, it means you are jealous. This idiom works because, figuratively, Paula the Pickle and Peter the Pear are very jealous of each other. The phrase also works literally since Paula the Pickle and Peter the Pear are, in fact, green vegetables. (Meanwhile, Tom the Tomato isn't jealous at all…and he isn't the color green.)

IT'S ONLY MILK

When you *cry over spilled milk*, you get upset about something that can't be changed. In this poem, Morgan doesn't get upset, so the idiom works figuratively. Of course, Morgan doesn't get upset about the spilled milk, so the phrase works literally, too.

LEFT FIELDER JALEN

The idiom *foul play* refers to something happening that seems inappropriate and/or dishonest. In this poem, Jalen commits *foul play* by stealing home plate. In this poem, Jalen also ends up sitting on home plate in foul territory, so the phrase *foul play* works literally, too.

POEMS WITH IDIOMS

ROVER'S BACKYARD

The idiom *the grass is always greener* is used when someone believes a different situation would be better than the current situation. In this poem, Rover is jealous of the dogs next door. Though the fence prevents him from seeing the other dogs' yard, Rover assumes their yard is much nicer than his yard. After the storm knocks down the fence, Rover notices that the neighbor's yard has brown patches all over the grass. So, it turns out, both literally and figuratively, that the grass (of the neighbor's yard) was*n't* greener.

GAME OF CARDS

If you *play the cards (or hand) you are dealt*, you deal with the not-so-great situation you are in. In this poem, Calvin and Sophie are, literally, dealt the same five cards (which are not very good). However, their reactions to this situation are quite different. Since Calvin gets upset when he sees his hand, he doesn't deal very well (figuratively) with the cards he was dealt (literally). Sophie, on the other hand (yes, that is also an idiom!), does handle the same situation much better.

POEMS WITH IDIOMS

SIMPLE MATH RIDDLE?

In this poem, Heather must pick two numbers off the floor that, when added together, equal four. Since she isn't allowed to pick up the number 1, there are only two possible combinations that could work: 0 and 4, or 2 and 2. Since there are no 0's, Heather's *only* solution is to, literally, pick up two 2's. Sounds like a simple math riddle, right? Well, not for poor Heather because she isn't able to figure it out. The idiom *put two and two together* means to figure something out with the information you are given. Unfortunately, Heather was unable to, either literally or figuratively, put 2 and 2 together.

CAVEMAN'S CONQUEST

The idiom *man of few words* means someone who says very little. The person may say very little for any number of reasons. Maybe he or she is shy? Maybe he or she prefers privacy? Whatever the reason, it's unlikely the reason he or she says very little is because he or she only knows a couple of words of the English language. Cavemen (and cavewomen, I suppose!), on the other hand, lived way back in the days of the dinosaurs, before there were many words in the English language. No wonder this caveman was, literally, a man of few words!

POEMS WITH IDIOMS

STEAK-ING HER CLAIM

When you get a *raw deal*, it means you feel like you have been treated unfairly. When the waiter brings Kate an undercooked steak, she tries to send it back. However, the waiter (and, later, the waiter's boss) refuses to cook her raw steak more. Even though Kate ultimately gets her steak for half price, which is a pretty good deal, she would have preferred it if they had simply cooked her raw steak more. Kate not only ends up with a raw steak, literally, but, since she isn't thrilled with the outcome, she also feels like she got a *raw deal*, figuratively.

TWIST AND SHOUT!

The idiom *all hands on deck* is used to describe situations where everybody must work together to accomplish a goal, often in a short amount of time. In this poem, the kids happen to be working together to accomplish their goal...which, of course, is to put all of their hands on the deck of the ship at the same time. Therefore, in this poem the kids are, both literally and figuratively, trying to get *all hands on deck*.

CIRCUS SHMIRCUS

The idiom *three-ring circus* means a noisy, out-of-control situation. The last line of this poem reads: 'Guess I was wrong to think there was a *three-ring circus* here.' This idiom works because, figuratively, none of the circus performers are doing anything, which makes it a quiet and boring situation. Of course, this phrase also works literally since this poem actually takes place at a circus.

POEMS WITH IDIOMS

WINDOW SHOPPING

The idiom *window shopping* is used to describe people who stand outside a store and look through the window at the merchandise without actually going inside the store and buying anything. When people hear the phrase *window shopping*, they almost always think of it figuratively. After all, it's pretty uncommon to actually go shopping for windows. In this poem, however, the Mom does love going shopping for windows, literally. The illustration, hopefully, reflects this, since the house has tons of windows (but no front door).

WORKING THE BOWLADROME

If something is *right up your alley*, it means you enjoy (and are probably good at) doing something. In this poem, none of the kids enjoyed working at the Bowladrome, so they ended up quitting for one reason or another. Sally, on the other hand, enjoys her job, so the idiom works here. Of course, Sally also happens to be working at the Bowladrome, where there are lots of bowling alleys (wooden lanes where a bowling ball is rolled on its way to the bowling pins), so this idiom is used here literally, too.

ALPHABET CATCHER

The idiom *catching some Z's* means getting some sleep. In this poem, the Alphabet Catcher is catching letters of the alphabet in her net, which is pretty tiring work. So tiring, in fact, that the Alphabet Catcher eventually falls asleep (*catches some Z's*). But what has caused her to be so tired? That's right...catching so many letters, including the letter Z's, in her net.

ANSWER KEY FOR ZANY WORD BLENDERS

#1
(things you wear)

vest
sandal
belt
hat
coat

#2
(kitchen items)

pots
plate
pan
soap
table

#3
(fruits)

pear
orange
lemon
melon
olive

CPSIA information can be obtained
at www.ICGtesting.com
Printed in the USA
FSHW04n1656140318
45438FS